Facts About the Honey Bee

By Lisa Strattin

© 2019 Lisa Strattin

Revised 2022 © Lisa Strattin

FREE BOOK

FREE FOR ALL SUBSCRIBERS

LisaStrattin.com/Subscribe-Here

BOX SET

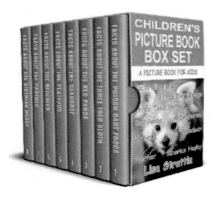

- **FACTS ABOUT THE POISON DART FROGS**
- **FACTS ABOUT THE THREE TOED SLOTH**
  - **FACTS ABOUT THE RED PANDA**
  - **FACTS ABOUT THE SEAHORSE**
  - **FACTS ABOUT THE PLATYPUS**
  - **FACTS ABOUT THE REINDEER**
  - **FACTS ABOUT THE PANTHER**
- **FACTS ABOUT THE SIBERIAN HUSKY**

LisaStrattin.com/BookBundle

Facts for Kids Picture Books by Lisa Strattin

Little Blue Penguin, Vol 92

Chipmunk, Vol 5

Frilled Lizard, Vol 39

Blue and Gold Macaw, Vol 13

Poison Dart Frogs, Vol 50

Blue Tarantula, Vol 115

African Elephants, Vol 8

Amur Leopard, Vol 89

Sabre Tooth Tiger, Vol 167

Baboon, Vol 174

Sign Up for New Release Emails Here

LisaStrattin.com/subscribe-here

★★COVER IMAGE★★

https://www.flickr.com/photos/hedera_baltica/51091524967/

★★ADDITIONAL IMAGES★★

https://www.flickr.com/photos/conall/51208256490/

https://www.flickr.com/photos/postmanpetecoluk/51320133292/

https://www.flickr.com/photos/sidm/51034780058/

https://www.flickr.com/photos/hedera_baltica/49706816058/

https://www.flickr.com/photos/stanzebla/52377231303/

https://www.flickr.com/photos/stanzebla/52394902220/

https://www.flickr.com/photos/hedera_baltica/51753401927/

https://www.flickr.com/photos/hedera_baltica/50254422983/

https://www.flickr.com/photos/137294100@N08/50042950868/

https://www.flickr.com/photos/hedera_baltica/51195953550/

Contents

INTRODUCTION

The Honey Bee is a small sized bee that inhabiting quiet forests, jungles, meadows, and gardens all over the world. There are only 7 recognized species of Honey Bee out of 20,000 different bee species found worldwide, but these individual species often contain their own subspecies. There are 44 known subspecies of the 7 species of Honey Bee.

CHARACTERISTICS

The Honey Bee is primarily involved in the production of honey and is today found worldwide. The Honey Bee is thought to originate from the jungles of south east Asia, where wild honey can still be found, and the Honey Bee eventually took up residence in a number of different countries in the world.

APPEARANCE

Honey Bees communicate with each other through a 'dance language' consisting of movements made by the Honey Bees' tail. They primarily use this form of communication to warm other Honey Bees of oncoming danger.

LIFE STAGES

The queen Honey Bee is the one who lays the eggs. She lays her eggs in a round-shaped mound that she then seals with wax. When the baby Honey Bees (larvae) hatch they must eat their way out of their sealed dome. Once they are out, they become a part of the system of pollinating plants, which is necessary for human survival!

Honey Bees are known to play a valuable part in the eco-system because around 1/3 of what humans eat is pollinated by bees. It is estimated that around 80% of the world's crop species are dependent on the pollination by bees to survive.

LIFE SPAN

The Honey Bee only lives for about 6 weeks.

SIZE

The bees are only about 1/2 inch long! They are not very big at all, especially considering how important their job is!

HABITAT

The Honey Bees build and live in a hive, run by their female queen who populates the hive. The Honey Bee collects nectar from flowers which it takes back to the hive to be turned into honey. At the height of the summer, over 40,000 Honey Bees can be found inhabiting just one hive. That's a lot of bees in one place!

DIET

The Honey Bee is a herbivorous animal and therefore lives purely on the nutrients from plants. Honey Bees prefer to ingest the sweeter plant produce such as nectar, pollen, and fruits, in order to make the honey.

ENEMIES

Due to their small size, Honey Bees have a number of predators in their natural environment. Birds, small mammals, reptiles, and other insects are known to prey on the Honey Bee; larger mammals, like bears, are notorious for destroying the hive of the Honey Bees in order to eat the honey inside.

SUITABILITY AS PETS

Honey Bees are not normally considered pets, although they are kept and cared for by beekeepers. This is so that we can harvest the honey they produce and protect them from extinction!

COLOR ME

COLOR ME

COLOR ME

COLOR ME

COLOR ME

COLOR ME

COLOR ME

COLOR ME

COLOR ME

COLOR ME

Please leave me a review here:

LisaStrattin.com/Review-Vol-184

For more Kindle Downloads Visit Lisa Strattin Author Page on Amazon Author Central

amazon.com/author/lisastrattin

To see upcoming titles, visit my website at LisaStrattin.com– most books available on Kindle!

LisaStrattin.com

FREE BOOK

FOR ALL SUBSCRIBERS – SIGN UP NOW

LisaStrattin.com/Subscribe-Here

LisaStrattin.com/Facebook

LisaStrattin.com/Youtube

Made in the USA
Las Vegas, NV
29 July 2023

75387581R00026